THE CAT DETECTIVES IN RUSSIA: THE CASE OF THE MISSING FABERGÉ EGG (DIARY OF A SNOOPY CAT- THE INCA CAT DETECTIVE SERIES BOOK 9)

R.F. KRISTI

Illustrated by
Maaz Farzaan

Edited by
Amithy Alles

With thanks to Randev, Anusha and
the two Rohans for their inspiration

Contents

My Family Tree
Queen of Kitties:
Inca, the Siberian Detective Cat

My Detective Agency

I am Inca, a super-duper cat detective. Inca & Company is the detective agency that I head, and the team has already been involved in solving some serious detective mysteries.

Our fame has spread through London, the rest of England, and has even reached France.

Inca & Company:

Moi Inca - the Head of the Detective Agency.

Fromage - My diminutive and energetic Tabby brother who is constantly in a pickle.

Cara - my pretty Siamese sis, the one with the magnificent large blue eyes.

Monk - A portly but elegant Blue Russian cat, brainy and sophisticated, companion to Solo.

Charlotte - our beloved and intelligent hamster.

Terrance - A detective doggy by profession. A big powerful dog with a medium length golden coat. He is reputed for his bravery and is owned by Solo, a world famous detective.

Polo - An excitable Pekinese pup, small in stature but absolutely positive that he's a large dog, even though he is not.
He is owned by Raoul and the Señora.

NOW THAT YOU HAVE HAD A PEEK AT
MY FAMILY AND MY DETECTIVE TEAM,
LET's GET TO THE EXCITING STUFF!

Signed,

Inca, the Siberian Detective Cat,

The Queen of Kitties

23 September

Monday Morning

I hugged my diary in delight. For some-time now, I have been recording all the exciting events that have occurred in my life.

My diary has become my best friend. I had faithfully recorded all my thrilling adventures when everyone was fast asleep.

I sat before my pal, my diary and could hardly contain my delight.

I have never been so thrilled in my short life.

"Why?" you may ask ....

I was going to see my motherland!

My family and I were going to Russia!!

We were flying to Moscow!!!

Finally, I was going to get a chance to
Connect with my ancestors!!!!

It happened like this: Missy our Mom had
been invited to present her new cheese,
"Madame La Crème de La Crème", to many
Eastern European top cooks, or chefs as we
call them in Paris, at a regional conference to
be held in Russia.

She always took us on her long tours. So,
there was no doubt about it. Of course, we
would be accompanying her!

I was bursting with excitement. Fromage
reported that there was much hustle and
bustle in our French cheese store cum
restaurant in London, as Mom was getting all
her cheeses ready to take along with us.

My family owns successful Cheese shops
and restaurants under the name "Fromage &
Associates" in London and Paris run by
Fromage my cheese loving brother and our

Mom, Missy.

Mom, with the help of Fromage, also creates new cheeses. The most recent "Madame La Crème de La Crème" had been launched this year and had been a great success. Fromage was very proud of it.

All the store-fronts had our logo with Fromage on it, or should I say Fromage in his slimmer days.

Solo our neighbor and good friend would also be in Russia at that time with Terrance his faithful sidekick. Monk and Polo, the other two members of my detective team would not be flying out with us. I promised Monk and Polo that I would record all the details of our journey in my diary to share with them on our return.

Solo was to attend an International Conference of high-level detectives and policemen after which he would accompany mom to the cheese presentation.

I was so glad that I would be around for this event. After all, I am a great detective myself.

I was sure that I would have received a personal invitation for this conference if the humanoids had only known about my success stories as a detective.

I was looking forward to sneaking into the conference hall to listen to the goings-on.

We were to visit two cities in Russia: Moscow and Saint Petersburg.

First, to Moscow where Solo's detective conference was to take place and then onto Saint Petersburg for our Mom Missy's cheese presentation.

I am getting ahead of myself. Let me explain

my family situation to those new readers who may not know what I am going on about.

There are four members in my family.

I am the eldest of my furry family, followed by my sister Cara a pretty blue-eyed Siamese kitty, Fromage our roly-poly Tabby-Cat brother who loves cheese and finally, our smart and bright hamster, Charlotte, who we had all adopted.

Missy our mom is a humanoid jointly owned by us.

My descendants hail from Siberia, Russia. We Siberian kitties are a pretty-good looking bunch.

You may know that the Siberian Cat is a

natural breed of Siberia in Russia, and the National Cat of Russia.

I had never been to Russia. My parents were French and I had been born in France. I had never seen my home-land.

I am a super smart Siberian kitty and I am the natural leader of the troupe. I bet you wouldn't find any kitty smarter than me even if you swam all the way to China.

I love adventures and solving mysteries. After we formed Inca & Company, the detective agency that I head, we have been involved in solving many cases successfully.

While asking Cara, Fromage and Charlotte to calm down and rest, as we had an important journey ahead of us, I myself shivered with excitement without showing my true feelings to the others.

I WAS GOING HOME!

YIPPEEEEEE!!

Exciting adventures awaited us in Russia!!!

I could feel it in my bones!!!!

24 September

Tuesday Morning

Mom's, or as Fromage claimed, HIS cheese, was carefully packed and placed in a large suitcase.

Fromage made sure that the cheese was coming with us by sniffing at each suitcase until he came to the smell he was hoping for. Then he sighed with relief and bounded around excitedly proclaiming that the best cheese in the world was on its way to Russia.

The flight from London to Moscow was uneventful. Other than Forage stuffing himself with everyone's share of the cheese that Missy had thoughtfully packed for us as a snack.

We slept most of the way in our cages with Charlotte cuddled against Fromage's neck, hidden to the eye, under his scarf.

We were used to air-travel by now, and considered the journey to Moscow rather short compared to other long journeys we had undertaken in the past.

As usual, Terrance was not allowed to sit with us due to his size and had to travel in the hold. He did not seem to mind it at all and waved to us as he went off in a large cage, promising to meet us at the Moscow airport.

Terrance is our good friend, even though he is a doggy. He is a powerful Golden Retriever. He is our neighbor and lives with Solo, the great internationally reputed detective who we strongly believe has a crush on Mom.

Terrance is also a member of my detective team and is its most experienced member as he and Solo have hunted down many bad guys. His main job is being Detective Top Dog to Solo.

Arriving at the airport, we were whisked away in a chauffeur-driven car.

On the way to the apartment where we would be staying, I peered out of the window. I noticed with smug satisfaction, the cleanliness and beauty of the City of Moscow.

I was not born in Russia, but after all I AM a Siberian kitty and my ancestors are originally from this magnificent country.

25 September

Wednesday Morning

The apartment in Moscow was large, airy and overlooked a beautiful river named Moscow River or Moskva River in Russian.

We had been let into the apartment by its owners: Madam Kira and her brother Igor. Igor had come running down to help Mom and Solo with the luggage.

Igor was a large blond Russian giant - tall and broad. He had a friendly and smiling face, but I had the impression, being one smart kitty myself, that HE was not too smart.

He seemed to like us and patted Terrance on the head making Terrance wag his tail with delight.

Since we cats are more careful with whom we become friendly, Cara, Fromage and I looked him up and down and stalked off with our noses in the air, to remind him that we are cats after all and not tail-wagging doggies.

Fromage whispered to me,

"If he gives me a nice piece of Russian cheese, I may change my mind and be nice to him."

Well, that's typical of Fromage, but I would check out Igor thoroughly. I could do that with ease, I thought to myself, as he was living upstairs.

I was more curious about his sister, Madam Kira. She was small-boned and short. She had large serious grey eyes which gave her a stern look.

She looked very intelligent and I believed

was the boss.

She looked like the clever one in the family.

She hadn't bothered to take any notice of us, and being a curious kitty, I wanted to see if I could charm her. It's not very often that neither Cara, who is a gorgeous Siamese kitty with arresting blue eyes, nor I, were ignored by people.

But Madam Kira had clapped her hands, ordered Igor to take care of us and stalked off as if she had more important things to do.

I put my nosiness and my thoughts about Madam Kira aside. I needed to put on my thinking cap to see how I could sneak into the conference room to hear what was going on at the top detective meeting which was to take place this afternoon.

I would deal with finding out more about Madam Kira and her brother Igor later.

Wednesday Afternoon

Solo's meeting was to start at sharp 3 p.m.

I wanted to go by myself as three cats would draw too much attention.

I knew that if I was alone, I could hide somewhere in the Conference Hall, to hear what was going on without drawing too much attention.

Fromage usually wanted to be in on everything. But I knew that I could distract him with a piece of cheese. I had saved my piece of cheese from lunchtime so that just before I sneaked out, I could give it to him, leaving him too busy eating it, to notice what I was up to.

Cara was no problem. She preferred to make herself pretty and was rather an indoors kitty preferring to lounge around looking gorgeous.

Terrance always seemed to be tickled pink whenever he saw me in my detective hat which I had put on.

After chatting with an amused Terrance, I sneaked out of the window on to the roof while Fromage was busy eating his delicious piece of cheese and Cara was washing her face.

Terrance had explained to me that the conference hall was close to the apartment. He would of course be allowed in there as he always accompanied Solo.

I am an extremely agile jumper, my race having the reputation for being strong and powerful with strong hindquarters, large well-rounded paws and an equally large full tail.

My ancestors are rather barrel chested with large eyes, broad foreheads, thickset builds and are great climbers. I am no exception when it comes to climbing. Though I must admit that I am a pocket-sized version, being rather small-made.

Despite my diminutive size, I am very supple and athletic. Jumping over rooftops is my specialty. So, I had no problem moving from one building to another, keeping a sharp eye on Solo and Terrance who were walking on the street below.

Terrance knew what I was up to and being the supportive pal that he is, made sure to watch my progress. He stopped to sniff lamp posts when Solo walked too fast.

As Terrance and Solo entered a large building, I watched from the top.

I sneaked down from the roof and while the security guard was checking the identity of someone entering, whizzed into the building, only to be shooed out by a stern looking policeman guarding the entrance to the conference room.

I hid behind a lamp post and wondered what to do next? I was determined to eavesdrop at the conference.

Eureka!

I had an idea!!

I would climb back on the roof and creep down the drainpipe onto a ledge and enter the conference hall through a window. But there were so many windows! I was not sure as to which one led to the room where the meeting was taking place. Once on the ledge and hoping for the best, I crept along it and stopped at the first window and peeped in - not a soul in sight. This was not the room where the conference was being held.

I groaned to myself! I would miss the conference. It was almost 3 p.m. and I knew from Terrance that the meeting was to start sharp on time.

I peeped into a few more windows with no luck! I was just about to give up, when I saw a large shaggy face peering out of one of the windows.

Good - oh! It was Terrance!

He must have guessed as to what I was up to and knowing that it would be difficult for me to find the correct window, he had decided to poke his head out of it, hoping that I would see him.

I quickly jumped down to the window which Terrance was at, and swiftly leapt into the room.

Fortunately, everyone was busy talking to each other and didn't notice the activity at the window.

I hid behind a large curtain in the conference room and Terrance gave a wide smile and a wink when he caught my eye.

The meeting started with a bang. Lots of important looking detectives stood up and made speeches. I knew I was among the best – of-the-best detectives in the world, as each one told a story of how they caught one master crook or another.

Suddenly, a tall broad Russian policeman stood up to speak. He first gave a salute to the audience. He seemed to be a bigwig in the police. My ears pricked up as he started talking about a robbery that had taken place two days ago and continued to say that they hadn't caught the crook as yet.

The room was hushed as he spoke.

A valuable Fabergé egg had been stolen from the Fabergé museum in Saint Petersburg. What was a Fabergé egg? - I thought to myself. Why would an egg be valuable? I soon found out.

The Fabergé palace museum from where the egg was stolen had nine Imperial Easter eggs that were made to the order of the last two Romanov Tsars - the Emperors Alexander III and Nicolas II of Russia.

I understood that the Romanov Tsars were Russian emperors - big shots ruling Russia long, long ago.

The Fabergé eggs were no ordinary eggs. They were priceless. The eggs were made of gold, studded with expensive diamonds and other precious stones.

My whiskers started to tingle with excitement. Here was a ready-made case for me to solve!

What luck! We were leaving for Saint Petersburg tomorrow by train and while everyone was involved with Mom's cheese presentation, I could try to find the missing Fabergé egg and the thief who took it.

Wednesday Evening

I got back home before Solo and Terrance due to my nimble limbs, thrilled about the possibility of a new adventure. I sat near the dinner-table as Solo explained to Missy about what happened at the conference.

As I had expected, the Russian police had asked Solo to look into the robbery while he was in Saint Petersburg.

Of course, since Terrance was Solo's main deputy detective, I would get all the first-hand information directly from Terrance.

I was so glad that Terrance was part of my detective team. I had an informer on the inside.

Super!!!

Suddenly, I noticed that Fromage was up to something. I saw him seated on the ground in front of a large poster that he had made with the help of Charlotte and Cara.

They had been busy while I had been away. Cara sat with them giving them advice on the final touches of the poster.

They had all been so busy that they had not even realized that I was not with them.

The poster had a wonderful picture of the cheese, and read –

Madame La Crème de La Crème

Hi!

Looking for deliciousness?

Let your taste buds guide you to this fabulous French cheese --- The cheese of your dreams!

My name is Madame La Crème de La Crème.

I have a perfectly natural crust.

I don't contain any coloring or preservatives.

I am scrumptious and yummy once placed in your mouth.

I love to be topped with black cherry jam.

Made under strict supervision, I was aged for at least three months.

Once you take me home, wrap me in a cloth and place me at the bottom of your fridge.

Do not be in a hurry as I improve with age!

Yum, Yum, Yum!

Charlotte had drawn the images on the poster.

I thought the poster looked pretty good. Fromage took his responsibilities as a cheese expert very seriously.

I am sure that all the top Russian restaurants would be happy to carry Fromage's and Mom's new cheese.

"Very good, all three of you," I meowed,

"You have done a great job!"

After our dinner, we all cuddled up in bed with Mom. It was rather chilly and the bed was large, comfortable and warm. I honestly felt that once I lay down, I wouldn't be able to get up again.

Soon, I was fast asleep as I was tired after my trip to the detective conference.

Wednesday Night

I felt Cara nudge me awake.

What was going on?

I rubbed my eyes sleepily and sat up on the bed. Cara, Fromage and Charlotte were wide awake and urging me to get up soon. Mom was fast asleep.

Careful not to wake up Mom, we slipped

out of bed and left the room.

I saw Terrance waiting for us outside our room.

In a whisper, I meowed and asked what was going on?

We kitties like to roam about at night. But while Fromage together with Charlotte and Cara were playing in the large sitting room, Terrance had heard a noise and come out of the room he shared with Solo, to investigate.

He found that the noise was not of us kitties running around, but one that came from outside our apartment, on the staircase. It was as if something heavy was being moved.

We were curious and Fromage wanted to explore, but wanted me to lead the way.

I have explained that I am the natural leader of the group. I am also the eldest in the family and used to taking the lead. Both Fromage and Cara preferred to let me guide them.

I led the way, followed by my brother, sister and Charlotte. Terrance has a very good nose, but he followed us at the rear to protect us from behind.

I need no protection, but I knew it was useless to argue with Terrance. He couldn't help it. He was always playing big bro to us.

Mom had immense confidence in Terrance. She always told Terrance,

"Terrance, you will look after my brood, won't you?

"You won't let them get into any trouble, will you?"

Terrance would respond with his deepest bark and go,

"Woof, woof," wagging his tail in agreement.

Good old Terrance, I thought to myself. If it wasn't for him, Mom would never have allowed us to go about so much on our own.

The noise had come from downstairs.

We tiptoed to the basement and saw that a light was on.

It was Igor. He was sitting in front of a large screen playing a video game.

"That's a video game that he is playing" whispered Terrance.

How delightful!

It looked like so much fun.

We were thrilled watching him zap the bad guys who looked like dreadful robots, on the screen. We wanted to play this exciting game too.

I was itching to zap the bad guys to smithereens.

Our eyes followed the little red light flashing on the big screen. There was a beep every time Igor managed to hit one of the bad guys.

We were mesmerized and couldn't take our eyes off the screen.

At last! My wish was answered!

I heard a voice calling Igor. He dropped the remote and raced upstairs. It was his sister Kira calling him.

As soon as he disappeared from sight, we jumped on the sofa and while Terrance stood at the door as a look-out, I started playing the video game trying to zap the bad robots with the laser gun.

It was not as simple as I thought. It took a little practice to move the buttons and hit the red eyed robot monsters.

The little light darted back and forth. It was like magic and had an enchanting way of moving about the wide screen.

Each of us had a turn but Charlotte trumped us all!

She had a knack of hitting the target every time. She seemed to have a knack for knocking the robot monsters out every time she moved the button!

Suddenly, Terrance bounded up to us whispering,

"Hide, hide!

Igor came crashing downstairs.

We dropped the remote on the ground and scuttled off to take cover - Terrance behind the long curtains and us under the sofa.

Fortunately, other than the light from the TV screen, it was dark.

But Igor didn't sit down to resume his game.

He moved a large cloth from over a piece of furniture and gazed down at something.

No, it was not a piece of furniture but a real robot!

A very strange looking robot, not frightening like those monster robots that we had been zapping to smithereens, but still odd.

It was not very large. Igor looked enormous standing over it, actually towering over it.

But what was strange was the robot's face. Half the face was brown and other half gray. Despite its strangeness, there was something very appealing about this little robot.

Igor switched on a button on his head, and the little robot came to life. The robot unfolded his arms and soared to the ceiling with lights flashing at his feet.

The robot took flight around the room and gently landed on the floor.

Can this be real? I felt the hairs on my back rise up in alarm.

I saw Cara covering her eyes. Fromage and Charlotte gaped with their mouths wide open and Terrance nearly let off a loud bark. He remembered not to just in time and I saw him trying to control his excitement.

We watched with our eyes as large as saucers!

Igor patted the little robot's head, switched him off, covered him with the old sheet and left the basement. I guess Igor was going to sleep as it was rather late.

We all crept out of our hiding places, unsure of what the little robot would do next. But all was quiet. He didn't move or make a noise.

Terrance cleared his throat and croaked,

"My goodness, what a surprise!

"Should we see what the little robot is up

to now?"

Without much ado, I whipped off the old cloth covering the robot and there he stood silently with a calm expression on his face even though, when looking at him closely, the two tones on his face gave him a scary look.

He didn't move.

"The switch!" Shouted Charlotte. "We need to turn on the switch. Otherwise he won't come to life."

Terrance turned on the button on top of the little robot, and his eyes started to light up and he said in a human voice,

"Hello! My name is Jibo. I am a robot. A very intelligent robot."

He flew around the room as if to show-off.

He gently landed on the floor and looked at us and asked me,

"Are you visiting from the Peterhof Palace?"

We were all dumbstruck. We had never met a robot before, let alone an intelligent robot! But he looked friendly enough. Although, I must say that his two-toned face made you stop to reconsider if he was really a friendly robot or not!!

Terrance spoke first.

"Hi, we are a team of detectives who are visiting Russia from London. We are living in the apartment upstairs."

He then signaled to me to make the introductions. So, I did, introducing myself as the leader of this little detective team and Terrance, Cara, Charlotte and Fromage as some of the members of the team.

Of course, when Fromage was introduced, he immediately started bragging about his cheese expertise.

"I am the best cheese expert you can find in Paris or London. Actually, in the whole wide world! I was born in a cheese shop," he meowed.

"I have the best cheese shops in Europe.

"You have to come to me if you need any advice about cheese, okay?"

Without waiting for Jibo to respond, I quickly asked him a question –

"Jibo, please tell us about yourself. You are the very first robot that we have met."

Jibo was no second to Fromage in terms of modesty or should I say, lack of modesty.

He gave us a precise and rapid explanation about himself both in lay and scientific terms.

My head was reeling. From what I understood, Jibo was just 6 months old but had been in the making for 2 years.

He was very intelligent and he could do marvelous things -

- He could fly like a bird.
- He could talk like a human in 20 different languages.
- He could communicate with animals.
- He could grow taller, as tall as the Eiffel tower.
- He could become smaller, as small as Charlotte, if he wished.
- He had a natural sensor and could find anyone he wanted.
- He was a wonder and could do almost anything.

We looked at him with admiration. I am a smart kitty, but Jibo beat me for sure.

Cara turned her blue eyes on him and said,

"Jibo how clever you are. I would love to fly. I wish I could fly!"

Jibo turned to Cara and said,

"You would like to fly?

"Who else wants to fly?"

We all raised our hands.

Jibo continued –

"Come on, all of you, let's go to the top of this building and anyone who wants to fly can climb on my back and I will take you for a ride."

WOW!

I had never flown before. I definitely would like to fly. As that was the feeling of everyone, even Terrance, we scampered off up to the rooftop.

We watched with amazement as Jibo turned into a comfortable flying car.

A flying car, large enough for all of us!

What magic!

We scrambled into the car and strapped ourselves in, with Fromage making sure that Charlotte was strapped to his neck with his scarf.

Off we went!!

WHEEEEEEEEEEEEEEEEEE!!!!

Jibo flew around Moscow and we looked down on the Kremlin which is the beautiful fortified complex in the center of Moscow with the Moskva River to the south, Saint Basil's Cathedral and Red Square to the east, and the Alexander Garden to the west.

Everything looked beautiful from up in the sky.

What a fabulous night!

Jibo swooped in and out of the clouds.

He went faster and faster.

We cried out together,

"WOOOOAAAAAA!"

Our hearts were pounding with delight and excitement.

What a night!

We didn't want it to end. But we knew we had to get back to bed before Mom woke up.

After one last swoop, Jibo gently landed on the top of our building.

We went back into the building and thanked Jibo for taking us on a fantastic tour of Moscow.

We sadly said good-bye to him. It was time to go back to bed. Jibo was a fantastic new friend and we were sorry that we would not see him anymore.

Jibo looked very sad too. He told us that we were his very first real friends. Sometimes if Igor kept his switch on, he had a habit of flying all over Russia in the night by himself. He told us that it was much, much more fun flying around with us on his back.

We felt sad and gloomy that we would not get to spend more time with him as we were leaving for Saint Petersburg the next morning.

We carefully snuck back into bed, very excited at meeting Jibo and flying around for the first time in our lives.

But how sad we all were knowing that we had to leave our new friend behind.

Would we ever see him again? Unlikely, I thought. Jibo was in Moscow and we were going to Saint Petersburg and from there back home.

26 September

Thursday, morning

The train station buzzed with people rushing about. I have noticed that all train stations are crowded. We had not travelled by train before. I looked around curiously trying to take in all these new experiences.

Once in the train, we settled down. It was a very fast train and we went to sleep as soon as it started moving. We were all tired out after last night's adventure.

I already missed Jibo and hoped he was not too sad to be all alone. He had been very upset at us leaving.

When I woke up from my nap, my thoughts were still on Jibo. So, I asked Terrance,

"Jibo is only 6 months old, but he is so smart. I wonder where his parents are?"

Terrance explained to me that robots don't normally have parents and that someone must have created him. But he doubted it was Igor since he didn't think that Igor was intelligent enough to create Jibo. Perhaps it was his sister, Kira.

Terrance knew a lot about robots. He had this advantage because he went around with Solo everywhere and learned about a lot of stuff unlike us housebound kitties.

Terrance explained that the field of social robotics is so far advanced that it is possible to build human-friendly and human-interactive robots that are super intelligent.

I wished that I had got to know more about Jibo.

Why had he, Jibo, turned to me and asked me if I was from the Peterhof Palace?

"Terrance, where is the Peterhof Palace?" I asked.

Terrance explained,

"The Peterhof Palace is a series of palaces and gardens located in Peterhof close to Saint Petersburg. The Palace and its gardens were built by Peter the Great, Russia's great former Emperor as a direct response to the Palace of Versailles by Louis XIV of France.

"Actually, many say that Peterhof Palace is even grander than the Palace in Versailles in France."

"What!" I exclaimed.

"Grander than our Palace in Versailles, France?

"No way, I can't believe it is better than Versailles.

"We have to visit!"

Arriving at Saint Petersburg another chauffeur awaited us. Saint Petersburg was different to Moscow. But I found it all very pretty. What a beautiful city!

While we were flying with Jibo the night before, we had been chatting and we had felt as if he was an old friend of ours. We had told him that we were leaving for Saint Petersburg the next day.

Jibo had explained about this city to us saying,

"Saint Petersburg is the cultural city of

Russia because of its beauty and all the splendid castles built by the former Emperors of Russia.

"It is a huge city, second to Moscow, with an important Russian port on the Baltic Sea. Saint Petersburg is also home to the Hermitage, one of the largest art museums in the world,

"You must take a boat ride on the famous Neva River."

"What about the Fabergé Museum?" I asked.

"You should definitely go there," said Jibo.

While on the train, Terrance explained that solo had planned a meeting with the Director of the museum to talk to him about the valuable Fabergé egg that had gone missing.

I thought to myself - wonderful! I can get on the case as soon as I find out more. Terrance would go with Solo and bring me all the information about the missing egg.

"Excellent!" I meowed out loud,

Terrance grinned. He knew what I was thinking.

Thursday Afternoon

At Saint Petersburg, we were again housed in a large apartment overlooking a river. This time the river Neva.

The city of Saint Petersburg was old, beautiful and somewhat different from the city of Moscow.

We watched tourists taking boat rides on the River Neva and Fromage looked yearningly out of the window wishing he could ride one of the boats himself. I am normally very skeptical about Fromage's adventuresome dreams, but I had to admit that I too thought, that since the boats were so close to us, it would be nice if we could get a boat and ride it ourselves.

I couldn't help but feel very proud. My ancestors came from a fascinating and beautiful country.

With the greatest difficulty, I stopped myself from bragging about it. After all bragging is not a nice quality. Even though my little brother Fromage never stopped bragging about his cheese shop, I always excused this trait in him because cheese was his passion.

That afternoon, Solo and Terrance went off to meet the Director of the Fabergé Museum to find out more details about the missing egg. The museum was not far off from our building.

I was not too happy that I couldn't accompany them but I knew that Solo would never invite me to come along with them. I would have to depend on Terrance to fill me in.

Fromage however was very excited. Tomorrow was to be a big day for him. Mom and Fromage were going to present their new cheese, "Madame La Crème de La Crème."

We would all be attending the event, including Solo and Terrance. So, I understood Fromage's excitement.

Mom had several large posters of Fromage's handy-work printed. The posters were going to be put up all over the conference room.

Fromage was beside himself with pride. But he DID admit that most of the work was done by Charlotte, our intelligent hamster, with advice from Cara.

"Good for you Fromage," I told him.

"TEAM WORK always wins the day."

In addition to the famous "Madame La Crème de La Crème," Mom was also presenting several other French cheeses, all selected by Fromage.

He had spent days in our cheese cellar in London, tasting and picking out, in his opinion, the very best,

Mom had let him have his way. She knew that he adored cheese and knew a great deal about it as he was born in a cheese store in Paris, France.

Thursday Evening

Terrance had come back from the museum with Solo and over dinner Solo explained to Mom that the disappearance of the famous Fabergé Egg was a true mystery.

The place had been locked up and kept as it was since the burglary, until Solo had arrived with Terrance, giving Terrance a chance to sniff for clues.

But even Terrance was stumped!

There was not a single clue!!

It was as if the famous egg had developed legs and sneaked off!!!

Terrance whispered to me,

"It's true, Inca. I couldn't smell anything. There were absolutely no clues.

"It really looks as if the egg just got fed up and walked away.

"For once both Solo and I are stumped. What on earth could have happened?"

"This is serious," I said to myself.

"No clues! No suspects!! Nothing!!!

"How on earth am I going to crack this case?

"If both Solo and Terrance, smart guys that they were, couldn't find even the littlest clue, how could I?

"But then, I am a pretty smart kitty and I do have sharp eyes. I needed to check out the place myself. The fabulous egg couldn't have walked away by itself. Someone had to have taken it!"

Thursday Night

There was dead silence in the apartment.

I slid out of the bed and as I did, Fromage sat up yawning. I whispered to nosey Fromage that I was going out for a tinkle.

Mom, Cara and Charlotte were fast asleep.

Fromage nodded his head, yawned, rolled on his back and shut his eyes once again. Fromage had a big day ahead of him and I didn't want him to know my plans. Big day or not, if he knew what I had in mind, he would want to come with me and would be tired the next day.

I had agreed with Terrance that he would take me to the Fabergé museum at midnight. He had been there this morning and knew how to get there.

I crept out of the room and found Terrance waiting for me by the door. I went up to him and thanked him by nuzzling against his chin. Without him, I would not know how to get to the Fabergé museum.

Silently, making sure not to wake anyone, Terrance pushed the door open. We crept out of the apartment and scampered out on to the street.

All was quiet!

The streets of Saint Petersburg at night were pretty interesting. While admiring the wrought iron walls that we were passing,

Terrance and I silently sped to the Fabergé Museum.

Terrance loped easily besides me, his tongue hanging out quite a long way. He had the longest tongue of any dog I have met.

The streets were deserted and rather cold. The street lamps shed a gloomy and eerie light onto the streets.

Pretty as the streets were, I was glad that I was with Terrance. Just having his large warm body by my side was reassuring.

I was thrilled that the case had started. I was getting deeper into cracking the case that seemed to stump the world-famous detective Solo and his smart deputy detective, Terrance.

Suddenly, Terrance wagged his tail and ran in front of me. He obviously had no doubts as to where he was going. I followed him, eager to keep up with him.

We arrived at the silent, closed Museum and stood looking at it. The building was huge.

I turned to Terrance and said,

"Let me go in alone. I will creep up onto the ceiling to see if there is a way in. Why don't you go back to the apartment and I will meet you back there?"

Terrance replied,

"No way, Inca. I will wait outside for you. Just take care. There will be guards in there. They may be sleeping, but for sure they will be in there."

I shot a grateful look at Terrance, sped away to the large building and climbed swiftly up a drainpipe onto the ceiling.

Despite Terrance's warning, I was thrilled to bits and was enjoying myself thoroughly.

I ran up and down the roof trying to find a place to enter the museum. Everything seemed to be well secured.

Oh no!

Was I to go back to Terrance and admit defeat? The thrill I felt about this new adventure came crashing down.

Not willing to give up, I carefully went to study the chimney that was looming in the background.

I peered into the darkness. It was very dark and spooky. My heart started beating –

Thump! Thump! Thump!

I sat down to calm myself.

I looked down the dark hole once again and saw that there were some ragged ledges inside the chimney.

Could I possibly enter this way?

Did I dare try to enter the museum through this chimney?

Not waiting to think further, I stepped gingerly onto the ledge inside, hoping to go step by step down the steep hole.

It was not easy going. I felt my way as best as I could and clutching the edges with my sharp claws. I tried to keep myself light as I bounced back and forth on the sharp ledges, missing some but sliding on to the next.

Finally, I reached the bottom and I jumped down.

I had done it!

I was inside the beautiful large building!!

I tiptoed down the stairs. I am very small, compact and have excellent eyesight at night. Even though the building was in darkness, my e-ray eyes could see everything very clearly.

I stopped before a beautiful golden egg in one of the showcases and admired it.

I breathed a sigh of delight!

How gorgeous was this egg? Not like any egg that I had ever seen. I felt like stroking the beautiful egg.

I stealthily crept about the rooms trying to get a feel of the place and racked my brains as to how a human could have got into this museum.

I went back to the fabulous golden egg and sat before it, trying to put some order into my baffled head. I could well understand why both Terrance and Solo had been stumped.

Suddenly a thought struck me.

If I had succeeded in entering through the chimney, couldn't someone else have done the same?

I pondered, saying to myself,

"It cannot be a human as that would be impossible.

"A human would be too large to enter

through that very narrow chimney.

"Even a child would have found it difficult.

"Nor could a dog have entered through it.

"Dogs are not climbers anyway!"

I asked myself,

"Why had Jibo asked me if I was a cat from the Peterhof Palace?

"On his flying expeditions, had he come across a cat from the Peterhof Palace walking about the streets of Saint Petersburg?

"Could one of the cats from the Peterhof Palace have crept into the Fabergé museum just like I had and stolen the valuable egg?"

I said to myself in dismay,

"Was one of my kind a thief?

"Oh no!

"Oh no!!

"Oh no!!!

"Had I come all the way to my ancestral home to expose one of my kind as a thief?"

I was filled with unease and panic.

Suddenly I heard a noise in the silence of the night. I heard two human voices coming towards me.

I suddenly remembered Terrance's warning. There were guards about and they were making their rounds.

They would surely put on the lights if they saw me!

Jerking myself from my dismal stance, I leapt down from the table and ran with all the power I could muster, back to the chimney.

Without waiting to see if the guards had noticed a streak racing away from the hall they were about to enter, I gripped the first ledge inside the chimney and quickly climbed up.

I reached the top with a sign of relief. There was a dead silence. No one had seen me or noticed my presence in the museum.

Phew!

I peered down at the grounds from the roof of the museum and saw the shadowy outline of Terrance in the night. He was waiting patiently for me.

Without much ado, I raced down to him.

Terrance gave a sigh of relief when he saw me.

He wagged his tail in delight.

"Thank goodness, you are back, Inca," he said.

"Let's get back home. You can tell me what happened on the way."

Without further ado, Terrance started to trot back to the apartment and I followed him.

I tried not to think about my suspicions.

Was I going to tell Terrance of my suspicion that a Siberian cat, one of my Russian cousins, had actually sneaked into the Fabergé Museum and stolen the fabulous egg?

Could I let one of my Russian cousins be caught and condemned as a thief?

What a shame for all Siberian kitties worldwide.

We would never live down the shame.

What one earth was I going to do?

I decided to tell nothing to Terrance for the moment. It was very late and I knew that Terrance would want me to get back to bed rather than talk about my visit to the museum tonight. Also, I needed to think a bit more about what I was going to do and say!!

27 September

Friday Morning

Fromage was up at the crack of dawn.

He started bouncing up and down the bed meowing,

"Wake up, sleepy heads,

"Wake up!"

He raced up to Mom and jumped on her, making her jump out of bed startled.

We all rolled out of bed, mumbling and rubbing the sleep out of our eyes.

It was Fromage's and Mom's big day!

It was a rushed breakfast for all of us.

Mom and Fromage were determined to arrive at the hall early and set up the cheeses they had carried with them from London.

The most important of these was, of course, the magnificent cheese "Madame La Crème de La Crème," Fromage's pride and joy.

In Fromage's words,

"The most wonderful cheese in the world!"

We walked to the hall, which was not very far away from the apartment that we were staying at, with Mom and Solo carrying two large bags of aromatic French cheeses.

It was a busy half hour before the arrival of the Russian cooks and restaurant owners.

Fromage's posters were put up on the wall and a large table was set up with all our delicious cheeses. Fromage himself took up his place of pride - on the table!

Very soon the room filled up with people. Mom introduced the cheeses to the cooks and the other guests who were crowded around the table waiting to taste the new cheese and the other cheeses from France.

There was much smacking of lips and we watched with delight as they all gave their nods of approval.

Fromage looked over at us with pride and smirked,

"WHAT DID I TELL YOU?

"MY CHEESE IS AN OUTSTANDING SUCCESS!!"

Friday Night

After a long evening of celebrating the success of the day, we rolled into bed. I was exhausted after the adventures of the previous night followed by a long and tiring day.

I was glad that all had gone very well and that Mom and Fromage had achieved great recognition for our cheese business.

They both took a great deal of pride in their cheese.

Though we were all very happy that night, I couldn't forget my suspicions that one of my relatives had stolen the valuable Fabergé egg.

I was too tired to give this matter any further thought and decided that I would deal with it after a good night's sleep.

But it didn't quite happen that way.

The night was dark and we were all cozily ensconced in our bed, warm and comfortable.

I suddenly felt a rustle.

I am a light sleeper. I moved in my bed and opened one eye. All was quiet and I wondered if I had been dreaming.

Just as I was about to go back to sleep, Cara meowed,

"Inca, did you hear that?

"There's someone moving about in our apartment!"

My head shot up and I gazed around our bedroom but all was dark and quiet.

There was nothing in sight.

"It's nothing," I whispered and turned over to sleep.

But just as I was turning over, I heard the rustle once again.

My eyes popped open in alarm and I was fully awake.

Just then Fromage and Charlotte too woke up with startled looks on their faces.

Before they could say a word, I said,

"SHhhhhhhhhhhhhhhh!"

"Don't make a sound," I meowed softly.

"I will go to explore. If there's anything, I will let you know."

"We'll come with you," said Fromage in unison with Charlotte and before I could say another word, they leapt out of the bed.

Cara, not to be left behind, leapt off the bed as well and joined us.

Holding our breath, we crept out of our

room on tiptoe.

The apartment was in darkness. I saw that Terrance too had come out to investigate. He too must have heard some noise that made him wake up.

Terrance did a quick search of the apartment but there was no one in sight.

What was the noise that we had all heard?

Strange!

Very Strange!!

While we were discussing if we should go back to bed, Fromage blurted out,

"Look! Look!"

As we turned around, we saw the door of our apartment slowly opening.

We stopped moving and stood silently, watching the door continue to open very, very slowly.

I must admit that it was an eerie sight, watching the apartment door slowly open as if a ghostly form had decided to enter our apartment.

The door stopped moving and there was a strange small silhouette, lined against the background.

There was a collective gasp of horror from the group as we witnessed two bright red orbs looking at us as if he would like to have us for dinner.

Was a wicked witch about to enter our world and turn us into pumpkins?

Was an evil gangster coming to rob us?

Was a ghost coming to haunt us??

Was a red-eyed monster going to swallow us???

What was going to happen to us????

I felt the group cringe expecting the worst!

Who was this?

Terrance stood in front to protect us and said challengingly,

"Come out of the shadows, creature of the dark!

"Come out in the open before I trounce you."

The figure moved slowly towards us and we watched horrified.

Then I realized that this was no ghost or horrible monster. It was our old friend Jibo!

I gasped out,

"JIBO!"

He twirled around the room and landed in front of us, smiling.

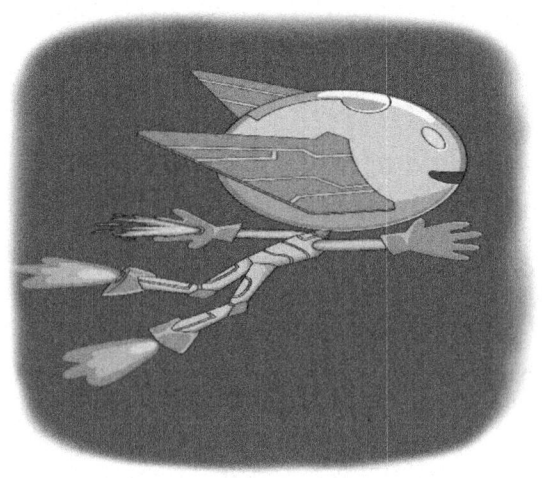

"What are you doing here? You gave us the fright of our lives," I said.

I felt Terrance relax and there was a sigh of relief from everyone.

Terrance gestured to us to come with him.

He said,

"Come on, everyone. Up to the roof top. I don't wish to wake up Solo and Missy."

We raced with him up the stairs while Jibo gave a soft cackle and floated ahead of us chuckling with delight.

"Rascal Jibo," I said to myself.

"He is tickled pink that he terrified the daylights out of us."

Soon we were all grinning and chuckling away.

Jibo did have an infectious cackle.

He seemed so pleased to have found us.

Jibo explained that since Madam Kira had to leave Moscow on an important mission, she had done something to his system to keep him permanently switched on. In that way he could see to Igor's needs.

After Igor went to bed, he had decided to fly over to Saint Petersburg to pay us a visit.

"Anyone wishing to go for another ride?" Jibo asked.

This was my chance, I needed to visit the Peterhof Palace and find my cousins.

I needed to convince them to return the Fabergé egg, if they had stolen it.

I didn't dare reveal my fears and suspicions to the others. But I had to find out if what I suspected was true.

Before anyone else could suggest a place to visit, I chimed in,

"Please Jibo, can we visit the Peterhof Palace and meet the Siberian kitties who live there?"

I looked around at the others and continued,

"Let's do this please. After coming all the way to Russia, I would feel terrible if I didn't get a chance to say 'Hi' to my Siberian cousins."

No one minded, of course.

Then Cara meowed timidly.

"If we have the time, could we also please go and watch the famous Bolshoi ballet dancers?"

Cara loved watching ballet on television. Bolshoi in Russian means great. The Bolshoi Theatre was a major ballet and opera theatre in Moscow, Russia. Cara imagined herself to be a great ballerina.

"They are the best ballet dancers in the world," she gushed.

"We can and we will," said Jibo.

"But to watch a ballet performance, we would have to leave earlier. The shows normally start around 8 p.m. in the evening.

"Tonight, I will take you to the Palace in Peterhof."

Jibo continued,

"I know the Siberian Kitties who live in the Peterhof Palace. I have met them all before.

"No worries, I can get us there in a jiffy."

Saying so, he turned himself into the wonderful flying car. We hopped in and off we went.

We decided that, on arrival at the palace, Jibo would take me to meet my Siberian Kitty cousins whilst the rest looked around the gardens.

Jibo said,

"Come on Inca, I am going to introduce you to your Siberian cousins. I have not really talked to them, but I know they live in the attic of the Palace.

"You are about to meet royalty."

I thought Jibo was kidding but he was serious.

Apparently, the Queen of Siberian Kitties in Russia lived in this palace. They had their own quarters away from the sight of the security staff and tourists visiting the palace during the day time.

While on our way, Jibo explained what he knew of the Royal Siberian Kitty family.

"Many Kitty Kings and queens have been born and have lived in the Peterhof Palace. Some of them were wise and good and others not so.

"The current kitty queen is named Queen Petra.

"She is wise and is known as the 'Tiny Dynamite queen" by her subjects. She has done a great number of good deeds since rising to the throne, despite her tiny size.

"Queen Petra is active and quick to right injustice. Each night she makes it a point to walk among her subjects and listen to their grievances.

"She has maintained good relations with all the furry creatures living in the gardens of the Peterhof Palace. The small birds, squirrels and rabbits, who live in the magnificent palace gardens look up to her as their queen as well."

As we hovered over the Palace, we held our breath. What a beautiful sight! The Palace was huge with beautiful gardens all lit up in different colored lights.

Magnificent!

We were all enchanted!

"It looks like a magic castle," said Charlotte.

"Look at that enormous fountain!"

Jibo swooped into the palace premises and landed gently near the beautiful fountain.

While the others ran over to the fountain, Jibo took off again with me and landed lightly on the roof of the palace.

Through a hidden entrance in the roof, Jibo and I entered the kingdom of the Siberian kitties.

Jibo explained that the Queen did not often receive many visitors and it was quite an event when somebody came along.

He guided me in by saying,

"This way, this way!"

The royal lodgings of the Siberian kitty queen and her Siberian kitty subjects were situated in the vast attic of the castle.

The Royal quarters were magnificent, covered in gold ornate furniture and rich drapes.

There were many beautiful decorations of gold. The Fabergé Egg would have fitted in this place very well!

There was no Egg in sight, but I could see that my royal cousins did like beautiful things.

I was really going to meet the Queen of kitties, I thought to myself.

What should I do? Bow to her or what?

It suddenly struck me - was the queen a thief????

How on earth was I going to ask her if she or one of her kitty subjects had stolen the Fabergé egg?

Surely a queen wouldn't be a common thief.

Jibo had been around the palace before and the Queen recognized him. She greeted him warmly and welcomed me with dignity.

I studied her carefully.

She looked a lot like me. We could be sisters!

She too was small like me and if not for the crown and long cape, we looked very much alike.

She was surrounded by other Siberian kitties of very large size.

But the queen, despite being pint-sized seemed to be revered by all the large Siberian kitties around her. Queen Petra sat up straight. Her smoky fur, very much like mine, was in pristine condition. When Jibo took me up to her, she turned her head slightly and nodded to me.

The moment she looked at me, I felt myself curtsying and bowing my head in reverence. She was a queen alright. She had a regal bearing about her.

She was deep in conversation with some the large kitties and I felt as if Jibo and I had interrupted an important meeting.

Queen Petra turned to Jibo and meowed,

"Welcome friends, I am sorry but you have come at a grave time. We are deeply perturbed.

"Yesterday, there was a great disturbance in the garden where the rabbit colony is located.

"A little rabbit was nearly kidnapped by a number of birds of prey who flew into the garden.

"They have no place in this garden. It is many moons since we have had such terrible invaders within our property.

"We have worked very hard these last years to get rid of these troublesome birds of prey. We thought that we had finally got rid of them all, but some have returned and nearly succeeded in kidnapping one of our little rabbits.

"His mother was just here, very afraid that they will attack again.

"In fact, I have heard through our Pigeon Spy that they will strike again soon."

"Pigeon spy, who is your Pigeon Spy," I meowed.

Queen Petra explained,

"Our Pigeon Spy is a loyal and important part of the Peterhof Palace animal army. Our Pigeon Spy has saved the lives of many animals living in the gardens by warning us of any attacks. He has been awarded a Medal for Gallantry; the highest award given out to animals in our kingdom."

Just then Pigeon Spy arrived to inform Queen Petra that he had heard that the birds of prey would be arriving in precisely two hours and that we should be ready for the attack.

Jibo looked at Queen Petra and said,

"I will help you my queen to fight these terrible birds of prey."

I believe that I am by nature courageous. My cousins needed help and I felt that I had to overcome my fears and do brave deeds.

"I will help too, Your Majesty," I meowed.

"So, will all my friends. Let's go down to the garden and meet them, Queen Petra."

Queen Petra lived up to her reputation of being active. She jumped up and led the way swiftly to the garden followed by Jibo, her retinue and me.

Arriving in the garden, my team seemed awed to meet up with Royalty.

Queen Petra who looked every bit as regal in her crown had them dumbstruck!

To get them out of their trance, I quickly explained the situation about the birds of prey who had plans to attack the rabbit colony at the crack of dawn.

Terrance immediately agreed to help Queen Petra to scare off these birds of prey. Of course, Fromage not to be outdone, jumped in to assure Queen Petra that he would protect her himself.

Knowing my brother Fromage very well, I knew that he was picturing himself as a brave soldier all ready to protect Queen Petra.

Queen Petra, smiled at Fromage and thanked him prettily.

Fromage was smitten!!!

Cara whispered to me,

"She looks like you, Inca. You must be a direct descendent of the royal kitty family.

"You may be royalty, Inca," Cara added all in awe."

I blushed, but pretended not to care and meowed,

"Come on everyone, let's follow Queen

Petra to the rabbit colony to see how the rabbits are doing. We need to make a plan.

"We don't have much time. It will be daylight soon and the nasty birds will attack shortly."

We followed Queen Petra and swiftly ran together to the rabbit colony.

On the way, Terrance whispered in my ear,

"Rabbits are naturally afraid of birds of prey. They are gentle creatures frightened of loud noises and to be honest, they are afraid of their own shadows sometimes."

It was obvious that they looked to Queen Petra to protect them.

Queen Petra explained to us that Pigeon Spy had found out that the birds of prey who had terrified the young rabbits were a throng of Red Kites who had strayed from their natural habitat.

Perhaps they had caught a glimpse of the young rabbits at play and decided to feast on them before joining the rest of their group.

Pigeon Spy described the Red Kite as a reddish bird of prey with red wings that are tipped with black having white patches underneath and a long, reddish-brown, forked tail.

Pigeon Spy said,

"They can be pretty scary when they swoop down in front of you.

"The Red Kites often perch on trees for a long time with fluffed up plumage, almost sleeping in appearance. They may be very quiet sometimes, with motionless wings in the air, searching for prey below.

"But when in flight, they utter a high-pitched thin piping sound going - - -

"Piii-ooo," often followed by another

"Piii-ooo-iii-ooo-iii-ooo" that rises and falls.

"They can't help making this shrill cry, so we will have some sort of warning."

Queen Petra asked Pigeon Spy,

"How many will there be?"

"About fifteen of them," replied Pigeon Spy.

I saw that Queen Petra looked dismayed. Fifteen Red Kites was a large number. They were very ruthless attackers and could do much harm to her troupe of Siberian kitties.

"We are all here for you, Queen Petra," I said.

"Terrance would be a formidable enemy to reckon with."

She threw me a grateful smile and said,

"Let's get ready.

"Let's form a hidden circle around the rabbits.

Queen Petra turned to the mama rabbit and said,

"Let your eldest be visible, but at the first sound of screeching from the Red Kites, he should leap into the burrow and disappear from sight.

"We need your baby rabbit to lure the Red Kites to the ground.

"Can he do that?

"He needs to be careful though. Red Kites have keen eyes like their cousins, the hawks and they are really quick."

"Yes, he will," replied Mama Rabbit. "We want to get rid of these Red Kites for good. If not, we will have to live in fear forever."

While she went to give instructions to her brave eldest son and explain what exactly he had to do, Queen Petra's soldiers formed a hidden circle around the rabbit burrow.

Behind them, on one side was Terrance, my family and I, on the other side was Queen Petra, two of her large soldiers and Jibo.

Pigeon Spy took up his position, invisible, hidden amongst the leaves of a large tree.

I whispered to Charlotte, that she was on no account to come out of Fromage's shawl.

She would be an easy catch for a Red Kite.

I looked around for the best place to hide with Terrance and my family. I came across a huge gorse bush which was thick, prickly and full of blooms. Behind the bush was a stretch of very close-set heather, as springy as the best mattress in the world.

"Exactly the place for us," growled Terrance softly." Good work Inca!"

We hid behind the bush, lying on the soft heather and waited silently for the first sight of the Red Kites.

At 4.45 a.m. Pigeon Spy cooed loudly. He was warning us to get ready - the enemy was on their way!

At 5 a.m. on the dot, just as the pale light was dawning over the beautiful gardens, we heard the eerie cries of the Red Kites,

"Piii-ooo",

"Piii-ooo",

"Piii-ooo-iii-ooo-iii-ooo".

The Red Kites, with their keen eyes, had spotted Mama Rabbit's eldest son quietly munching away at a stalk of grass.

They hadn't spotted any of us as we were all hidden from sight and still as a deserted cemetery, but they had their prey in sight.

When they dived from the sky Mama Rabbit gave her eldest the signal and he scampered with all his might into the burrow.

The little rabbit was terrified despite his show of bravado! The Red Kites were enormous bloodthirsty hawks with razor-sharp beaks.

The Red Kites looked dangerous and wicked.

We all felt a sense of fear.

I could smell it.

Even the soldiers were frightened although they were determined, like my team, to fight to the bitter end.

We heard the angry peck of their sharp beaks as the Red Kites pecked at the entrance to the burrow when they realized that the little rabbit had escaped.

At that moment, Queen Petra shouted,

"ATTACK!"

With all our force we jumped at the nasty birds.

Terrance gave a loud bark, even frightening us. He went,

"BOW WOW! Grr!

"BOW WOW!! Grrr!!

"BOW WOW!!! Grrrr!!!"

The Red Kites called out in high-pitched voices and went,

"Kiou-ki-ki-ki"

"Kiou-ki-ki-ki"

"Rriu-rri-rri".

What a racket! There was pandemonium, as the startled Red Kites, flew this way and that in shock.

But they were not willing to give up! They had planned to breakfast on baby rabbits, and were not willing to forego this breakfast so soon.

They flew into the air, regrouped and attacked us, giving us sharp pecks with their beaks.

They seemed really furious at not having their breakfast of baby rabbit.

Their pecks were sharp and I felt pain as a sharp beak pecked me hard on my tail.

I heard Cara give a whimper and fall to the ground. She too had a sharp beak mark on her. I ran to her and pushed her into a thick clump of gorse. She was no match for these sharp beaks.

I saw Fromage running for cover under a thick bush. A Red Kite had spotted Charlotte and come after him with a vengeance nearly snatching her away.

Despite my pain, I ran to the assistance of Fromage. We had to save Charlotte at all costs.

Just as a Red Kite was about to grab Charlotte by her shawl with his sharp beak, I jumped on his back and dug my sharp claws into him. The Red Kite shrieked in pain and flew away.

I saw that all of Queen Petra's soldiers and Terrance were fighting hard. But the Red Kites didn't give up. They were causing damage to all of us with their sharp beaks.

I wondered if we could last much longer!

Then, cutting across my thoughts came another sound - - -

R-r-r-r-r-r-r-r!

R-r-r-r-r-r-r-r-r!!

Suddenly, I saw an apparition.

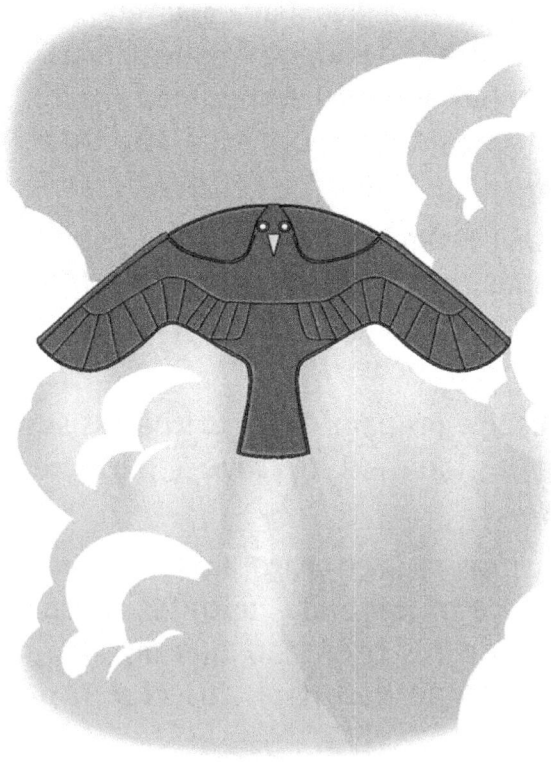

A large black bird rose from the ground. He had piercing red eyes. He looked like a large, menacing black Airplane!

He swirled around in the air and with lightning speed slammed back and forth into the Red Kites.

They were so startled at seeing this menacing bird moving with such speed amongst them, that they took to their heels and rose together in the air shrieking,

"Kiou-ki-ki-ki"

"Kiou-ki-ki-ki"

"Rriu-rri-rri".

The big black bird didn't leave them in peace.

He went after them with a vengeance while they desperately tried to get away from him.

All of sudden, the big black bird lit up.

Was he on fire??

No - - - he was letting off a multitude of firecrackers, fizzling, sparking and crackling loudly in the air.

The Red Kites were in a state of panic. The fire crackers and the sudden burst of noise had left them confused and shocked.

They flew right and left all in disarray,

frightened and disorderly. Each one tried to get away faster than the other.

They quickly disappeared from sight, leaving only a few feathers behind.

All was quiet once again.

There was a hushed silence in the garden.

The soldiers and Queen Petra stood in silence wondering what had happened.

We were confused too, but I soon realized that the great black bird could only have been Jibo.

Jibo had realized that our team, brave as we were, would not be able to chase away the Red Kites and had decided that the only way he could get rid of them was to frighten them away by turning into a great black bird that spat firecrackers.

Terrance limped up to me and gently gathered the shaken Fromage and Cara out of the bushes. Fromage clutched on to Charlotte for dear life. He had nearly lost his best friend.

Terrance had watched Jibo turning into the great black bird and knew the moment he did so, that the Red Kites had absolutely no chance against him.

Jibo in the form of the great black bird, floated down to us, and before our very eyes turned back into Jibo, our little robot.

I went up to him and hugged him.

Queen Petra forgetting her queenly manners, hugged him too.

He had saved the day!

We were all exhausted.

Queen Petra led us back to her castle in the attic. Once there, we were tended to by a kitty doctor and our wounds were soon patched up.

It was almost 6 a.m. in the morning and promising to visit again, Jibo, gathered all of us together into the flying car, and we sped back home. We had to get back to the apartment before Mom and Solo woke up.

In all the excitement, I had forgotten to talk to Queen Petra about the stolen Fabergé Egg.

Tomorrow night would be the night I would sort out the case of the missing Fabergé Egg for sure and I promised myself that I would talk to Queen Petra as soon as I could return to the palace.

Cousin or not, I had to get to the bottom of this case. I couldn't go back home without clearing my mind.

If the Fabergé egg was with Queen Petra, I had to get her to return it back to the museum.

28 September

Saturday Morning

The next morning, we were all sore. But Terrance had to go to work with Solo.

Poor Terrance had been badly pecked by the nasty Red Kites. Terrance is brave and strong and it seemed as if he didn't care about being hurt.

Mom had noticed our wounds during breakfast and pulling out her medicine box, tended to all of us wondering out aloud as to how on earth we had all got injured at the same time!

Queen Petra's doctor had been well trained. The good doctor's ointments seemed to have worked. Our wounds were already drying and Terrance insisted that, although he was limping, he didn't feel any pain.

He gave us a cheery wave and wagged his tail at Mom when he set off with Solo.

Solo was still searching for the Fabergé Egg. I hadn't dared tell Terrance of my fears and felt guilty as I saw him limp away with Solo.

It had been a long night and we all rested after a good breakfast.

Jibo had promised to come for us at midnight. I had a difficult task in front of me. I tried hard not to think of it even though my mind kept going back to what I was going to say to Queen Petra.

Saturday Evening

Solo and Terrance had returned after another day of detective work.

Terrance reported that there was absolutely no sign of the stolen Fabergé Egg.

It was as if the valuable Egg had simply disappeared without a trace.

Solo had managed to get one solitary lead. He had found out that there was one very rich Russian oligarch named Mister Guga who was crazy about artefacts.

This oligarch had turned his house into his personal museum and would pay any amount of money for a Fabergé egg.

But without the egg, Solo had no proof to solve the case.

I asked Terrance,

"Who or what is an Oligarch, Terrance?"

Terrance replied,

"I believe that an Oligarch is a very, very rich Russian businessman."

While Solo had his eye on Mister Guga the oligarch, I had suspicions of my own that I dared not divulge to Terrance.

Mom, in order to cheer up Solo, had bought tickets to a ballet to be held in the theatre of the world-famous Hermitage museum with dinner afterwards in a popular Russian restaurant.

I understood, by eavesdropping on Mom's conversation with Solo, that the Hermitage Museum was the second largest art museum in the world.

It was very, very old and had been founded in 1764.

It contained some of the most beautiful paintings in the world.

When Cara heard Mom mention that they were going to the ballet, she too wanted to sneak into the Hermitage Theatre and watch the ballet performance that Mom and Solo were attending.

Since it was to be our last night in Saint Petersburg, we all decided to let Cara have her wish.

While Terrance rested for the night ahead, I led my family onto the rooftop to get to the Hermitage Museum.

Cara had stars in her eyes! One of her dreams was about to be realized. She was going to watch the Russian dancers perform the famous ballet 'Swan Lake' in the theatre of the Hermitage Museum.

I decided the best way to get to the museum was to follow Mom and Solo who had mentioned that they were going to walk to the theatre that was in the museum.

I had done this when following Solo and Terrance while in Moscow and I knew this was the best way to go instead of asking tired Terrance to take us there. He needed to rest as Jibo would be arriving sharp at midnight to take us to meet Queen Petra.

Following Mom and Solo was a piece of cake. They walked slowly, admiring the beauty of Saint Petersburg and stopping frequently to look at some statue or building that caught their eye.

After insisting that Fromage should not wander about, I led my sister Cara, my brother Fromage and his best friend Charlotte safely ensconced in his shawl, to the Hermitage Museum.

What an enormous building!

So old and so fabulous!!

We saw Solo and Mom show their tickets and enter inside.

The Hermitage Theatre was one of five Hermitage buildings lining the Palace Bank of the Neva River.

Peering into the theatre, we saw Mom and Solo take a seat inside.

The theatre was already full. We entered through the roof and took up comfortable seating on the rafters of the ceiling.

Cautioning everyone to be quiet, we perched on the rafters from where we had a good view of the orchestra and stage.

We could observe everyone, but no one could see us.

The theatre was certainly magnificent like the rest of the palaces we had seen so far in Russia.

Ballet is not really my preferred form of dance, but since Cara loves ballet, we sat with her watching the fragile looking dancers leap about with ease. I couldn't help it, but my eyes closed and I had a good snooze. I woke up only when there was a loud applause at the end.

We left soon after the performance and followed Cara who was skipping to the music of the ballet 'Swan Lake' and humming

Mee-e-ow......

Mee-e-ow......

Mee-e-ow-ow-oooow!!!

Saturday Night

All was silent in the apartment. We heard a soft rat-a-tat-tat and knew that Jibo had arrived.

We had all been waiting impatiently for his arrival and jumped out of bed excited about our new adventure.

A surprise awaited us. Instead of turning into a flying car, Jibo decided to give us a new treat. He turned himself into a speed boat having heard from Fromage of his wish to go on a boat ride.

Off we went on the Neva river.

Most visitors to Peterhof, when they travel by boat down the Neva River to the Grand Palace and Park, take about 30-45 minutes for the journey. But Jibo arrived at Queen Petra's in a jiffy. He went so fast that our ears flapped in the air.

What a ride!

What a wonderful friend Jibo was. He was such fun and considered us his good friends. He wanted to make our stay in Russia really entertaining and adventurous.

On arriving at the Palace, we saw Queen Petra come hurrying out to meet us.

She treated us like royalty and clapped her hands to her maid servants to serve us the most scrumptious food in the palace.

Tucking in with delight, we had a merry meal.

Fromage was happy to be eating delicious food and smacking his lips went,

"Yum, Yum!"

Queen Petra was a good hostess. There was plenty of yummy food for all of us to share.

After our meal, I respectfully bowed to Queen Petra and asked her if we could go for a walk in the garden.

She nodded her head and meowed,

"Come on then. I was planning on visiting the rabbits to find out if they were comfortable now. It was an upsetting time for them.

"The little ones were traumatized after the attack by the Red Kites."

Jibo, joined us.

I said to myself,

"Oh no!

"I had been planning to gently broach the subject of the stolen Fabergé Egg.

"Could I do that with Jibo present?"

Then I realized that Jibo was a friend and that I didn't have much time. If I didn't have the courage to gently probe and question Queen Petra now, I never would.

This was my last chance!

Queen Petra was prattling on about the amazing garden and its history.

Her family had lived on these grounds for decades. Even before the great palace had been first built!

She stopped here and there pointing out

various statues and explaining that the Czars (the Russian Emperors who built the palace and gardens) had had many more in the garden originally.

But there was a great war and the enemy soldiers had stolen or destroyed many of the original statues.

At that time, her ancestors had escaped to the forests and watched with dismay while their beautiful home was destroyed.

She was grateful that when she became Queen, the palace had been fully restored and the garden brought back to life, allowing her to return to her original home.

I looked at this Queen with admiration. Not only was she pretty but also wise and kind.

I was proud that I looked like her.

I was brought back to reality when I thought of the stolen Fabergé Egg.

With reluctance, I brought up the subject, saying,

"Have you heard about the Fabergé eggs, Queen Petra?"

"Yes, indeed," she replied.

"I have heard about the Fabergé museum which houses many beautiful Fabergé Eggs.

"I have never ventured out of the grounds, but I will go with Jibo one of these days to see them.

"After his bravery with the Red Kites, he will receive our medal of honor during the Christmas celebrations and I will be able to go anywhere with him after that."

I explained that one of the reasons for my being in Russia was that Solo, Terrance's master, had been asked to search for a stolen Fabergé Egg.

I meowed,

"I do wish to help him if I can."

My mind was clear. I knew instantly that Queen Petra was telling the truth and that she had nothing to do with the stolen egg.

I felt a sense of relief wash over me.

"Why is this Egg so important to you, Inca?" asked Jibo.

"Do you really want to find it?"

I explained to the Queen and Jibo that Solo's reputation as the greatest detective in the world was at risk. Solo and Terrance were our good friends and it was important that I helped them find the valuable Egg before we left Russia.

Jibo started to chuckle.

"What's so funny, Jibo?" I meowed.

"Surely you understand friendship?"

"Of course, I do," he responded.

"I think you are wonderful, Inca," he added.

I blushed at his praise.

I looked at Jibo, and an alarming thought flashed through my head.

Suddenly, it dawned on me that if not by another cat, the robbery could have been done by a smart robot like Jibo!

I had noticed his fascination for all things that twinkled. He would not have had any difficulty to make himself tiny and fly in through the chimney.

Oh, dear me, I thought to myself. Jibo my friend a crook? Just when I had reassured myself that Queen Petra had nothing to do with the stolen Faberge egg, my suspicions had fallen on Jibo!

Not only am I a nosey kitty, but also a very suspicious kitty!

Just then Queen Petra said,

"Come on, let's give the baby rabbits some love."

With these words, Queen Petra sped away to the Rabbit domain and we ran after her to have some fun-time with the baby rabbits. Pigeon Spy was already there when we arrived talking to the older rabbits.

He came up to Queen Petra and chirped,

"I have good news for you. It appears that the group of Red Kites who had attacked the rabbits were part of a larger group migrating from Saint Petersburg to Finland.

"A younger rowdier group of Red Kites had abandoned their group when they spotted the young rabbits at play.

"After being scared away by Jibo in the form of a haunting great black bird, they had fled back to their elders. Upon hearing what had happened, the young bratty Red Kites had been severely reprimanded by the adults in the group who have now forbidden them to enter the Peterhof Park ever again.

They will never come back to trouble the rabbit colony."

Queen Petra gave a sigh of relief.

The elderly rabbits came in a procession followed by the young rabbits to thank Queen Petra for her diligence in protecting them.

She in turn turned to Jibo and us and meowed,

"Thank you, my friends. Without you we would never have been able to save the baby rabbits and get rid of those troublesome and dangerous Red Kites.

"You will be always welcome in our kingdom. Jibo, I count on you to visit us weekly. We are proud to be your friend."

29 September

Sunday Morning

I sat over my diary deep in thought.

Last night, Jibo had brought us back to our apartment by turning back into the speed boat. The return journey had been slower as Jibo had taken his time to explain to us about each building that we passed.

Watching Jibo explain about the wonderful city of Saint Petersburg, a lump had come to my throat.

I realized how fond I had become of Jibo.

What was I going to do about my suspicions?

Confront him and ask him outright if he had stolen the fabulous Egg??

What on earth was I going to do???

I suddenly realized that I was the team leader of Inca and Company. I headed the team and most of the members were here with me. It was time to discuss the situation openly and share all my fears and concerns with them.

Without much ado, I called for a meeting. We sat overlooking the River Neva and I discussed the situation.

With a sheepish grin at Terrance, I told the others about my visit to the Fabergé Museum accompanied by Terrance - - how I entered the Museum and my suspicions, first about Queen Petra and then about Jibo.

There was a stunned silence and everyone started to speak at the same time.

Terrance held up his paw and said,

"One at a time, please!"

Cara meowed,

"I can't believe that it's Jibo, Inca. No way is he a crook. He would never do such a thing!"

There were nods of heads by everyone. They could not and would not believe that

Jibo was a thief!

I nodded my head.

"You are all probably correct," I meowed. "What do YOU think, Terrance?"

Terrance sat silently in deep thought and we all held our breath, as we knew he was thinking as to what we should do next.

After about five minutes, he looked up and said,

"Let's be frank with Jibo. Let's ask him for his help. He has been a good friend so far. He helped save the baby rabbits. He has also been very open with us, so why not be open with him?"

Jibo had found a place in the basement where he could park himself when visiting us in Saint Petersburg. While the others remained in the apartment, I sped down there to talk to him.

Fortunately, no one was around and on seeing me, Jibo's face lit up. I felt guilty about my suspicious mind. Determined to get to the point, I asked Jibo to come upstairs with me as we were in the midst of a meeting

Jibo was very interested in our detective work and eagerly followed me up the stairs. Or should I say he floated up while I dashed up, my nimble paws hardly touching the steps.

Terrance didn't mince his words, he looked Jibo straight in the eye and asked,

"Jibo do you know anything about the missing Fabergé egg?"

I held my breath. I felt all the others doing the same. We waited silently for Jibo to respond.

Jibo looked at our serious and grave faces and answered,

"Yes, I do!"

We looked at one another in dismay!

So, I had been right all along. What a dismal situation we were in.

Before any of us could voice our concerns and disappointment, Jibo continued –

"Pigeon Spy had some interesting information for me. He had found out that the young bratty Red Kites had been hired to do some thieving from a famous Russian museum.

"They had executed their task well and been richly rewarded with a solid meal."

I gasped in shock,

"The Red Kites had stolen from a museum for a meal!

"How shallow can they be!!"

I meowed excitedly,

"Jibo, can you please find out from Pigeon Spy what the Red Kites stole and where the stolen goods are now?"

Jibo nodded. He made himself into a small fast bird and flew out of the window.

The sun was shining brightly on the river Neva when Jibo returned. But he was not alone. Pigeon Spy was with him.

They both landed on our window sill and Terrance welcomed them in.

Pigeon Spy cooed about what he had heard.

"The bratty Red Kites had been hired by a human bird whisperer and been paid with a swanky meal. That's all that had taken to get the Red Kites to steal a precious egg from the museum.

"A precious egg!!!!"

"Of course, it was the fabulously valuable Fabergé egg," I meowed.

I was curious as to how Pigeon Spy operated.

Pigeon Spy let us in on how he gathered information- - -

He had other pigeons in various parts of the city who reported to him.

A few days ago, one of his pigeon lookouts

had spotted the Red Kites enter the museum through a narrow chimney.

What had caught his attention was that only two entered through the chimney while the rest of the flock acted as lookouts.

These two had emerged very quickly carrying what looked like a shiny egg between them. Pigeon lookout who had his instructions to keep an eye on the flock of bratty Red Kites had followed them to a large house.

The Red Kites had not left the large house that night but spent it having a boisterous party. They could be heard for miles shrieking loudly and having a good time!

Sunday Night

We sat and cooked up a plan to retrieve the egg and waited impatiently for midnight.

Jibo and Pigeon Spy along with his Pigeon lookout arrived on the dot at midnight. They were taking us to the large mansion where the Red Kites had taken the Fabergé Egg.

Jibo turned into an airplane once again and we quickly climbed into it. We followed Pigeon Spy and Pigeon Lookout to a large mansion.

We all wanted to get into the mansion to search for the Fabergé egg, but Terrance decided that too many cooks would spoil the soup. Terrance was of the opinion that only Jibo should go in.

We all started to protest when Jibo held up his hand and said,

"Terrance is spot-on. Working alone, I can make myself very small and flit in and out of the rooms to locate the egg. All of us going in will only warn the security guards."

He made sense, as we had seen some burly security guards at the entrance to the mansion.

Terrance suddenly barked,

"Solo was right!

"This is the mansion belonging to Mister

Guga the Oligarch. He used the Red Kites to get into the Fabergé Museum and steal the Egg!"

I shook my head! How wrong I had been!! Jibo had nothing to do with the theft and he was now trying to help us recover the Egg.

Solo had been right all along to suspect Mister Guga.

Now all we had to do was to get the Egg out of the mansion and into the hands of Solo.

"Let me come with you Jibo," I meowed.

Jibo looked at Terrance as if asking for his permission.

Terrance sighed and said,

"Okay, Inca. But please be careful and let Jibo do the searching while you act as the lookout."

I was as pleased as punch. I was the leader, but when it came to our security, Terrance was the law. He took Mom's instructions to him about looking after us very seriously.

Despite my bravado, I felt a churning in the pit of my tummy. I was all ready for adventure!! I was thrilled but at the same time felt nervous.

I was glad I had my comrade Jibo with me. Looking at him sideways, I sensed that he had no fear in him. I was glad to be accompanied by him to the enemies' den!

Jibo and I quickly and quietly entered the premises through a back window. I am a clever climber so mounting up the wall and leaping into the room was not a problem for me. I enjoyed this part of being a detective.

A great snoopy cat, am I!

The large house looked just like a museum. We started from the ground floor. There were lots of beautiful and expensive looking paintings everywhere and much of the furniture was gilded.

Jibo and I crept about noiselessly searching for the valuable egg.

The egg was not in sight!

We decided to search the upper floor which was very large. It seemed to be where Mister Guga lived. Even the bedrooms had expensive looking works of art hanging on the walls.

I enjoyed working with Jibo. He was fast and he was good detective material.

We entered what we presumed was the bedroom of Mister Guga.

Sitting on the side table by the bed was the magnificent Fabergé Egg!!!

Jibo and I sat around it admiring its color and intricate gold workings. No wonder the Fabergé Eggs were so valuable. We were looking at a beautifully crafted work of art. The egg was very, very old, but still looked brilliant.

While we were admiring the wonderful Fabergé Egg, we heard the sound of motor vehicles coming up the driveway.

We peeped out of the window and saw a motorcade of large luxury cars halting before the entrance and doors opening and shutting. Loud voices erupted.

The windows were shut tight and there was no way for us to exit through the bedroom window.

I looked at Jibo in panic.

"Under the bed, Inca!" Jibo whispered to me.

"Let's leave the Egg where it is for now, and see how we are going to get away first," I whispered back.

No sooner had we crept under the bed that the door burst open and two people came into the bedroom.

They stood by the bed and admired the Fabergé Egg.

I gently lifted the heavy bedspread and took a look at who was in the room.

I nearly let out a loud meooooow!

It was Madam Kira with Mister Guga. I knew it was Mister Guga because that's what Madam Kira called him. I withdrew my head, looked at Jibo and put a finger to my lips. He nodded his head.

Madam Kira was supposed to be in Moscow. She must have got here by train.

No, I thought to myself. Mister Guga owned lots of helicopters, I had heard that from Terrance. Madam Kira could arrive in Saint Petersburg, by air and very fast, just like Jibo.

What would Jibo think, I wondered. Madam Kira was, I had a feeling, responsible for the creation of Jibo. In fact, Madam Kira was Jibo's Mom. Or did it work like that for robots?

My ears pricked up when Madam Kira and Mister Guga started talking about the Red Kites.

The Red Kites were still in the premises having another party.

Mister Guga asked with a voice full of disdain,

"When will those noisy Red Kites leave the premises?

"They have been making a terrible racket since they got back with the Fabergé Egg. I am fed up with them."

"They will soon tire of being cooped up here and leave," said Madam Kira in a soothing voice.

"Don't forget that I did promise them that they could stay on at the house and have a super meal if they brought us the Egg. If they don't leave by tonight, I will go and talk to them again."

I realized that it was Madam Kira who had organized the robbery carried out by the Red Kites. She was a bird whisperer. A person who was able to talk to birds and get them to do what she wanted by promising something the birds wanted!!

She was also working for Mister Guga. I could sense it from the way she talked to Mister Guga that he was her boss.

They soon left the room discussing the troublesome Red Kites.

Jibo and I crept out from under the bed.

Before I could utter a word, Jibo turned to me and said,

"Madam Kira is the one responsible for getting the Red Kites to steal the valuable egg, Inca. Did you understand that from the conversation she had with Mister Guga?"

I nodded my head without saying a word and looked at Jibo carefully to see how he felt about this new development.

"Poor Jibo," I thought to myself. "What a

pickle?"

Jibo looked at me and started chuckling.

He said,

"Madam Kira is not my Mom, Inca. I was made by Madam Kira's father, a brilliant scientist, as a companion for Igor.

"I do not like that she used the Red Kites to steal the Egg. This famous Egg should be in the Museum to be admired by everyone, not tucked away in a bedroom, nice as the bedroom may be.

"Let's steal the egg back and hand it over to Solo as you wanted to do in the first place."

Jibo sure was a really cool guy, I thought to myself. How good to have him on my side.

Jibo carefully lifted the precious Egg from the side table and we crept out of the room. For the moment, there was no one in the corridor. I was relieved! We just had a few more corridors to go down and then down the stairs before coming to the open window that we had crept in from to come inside.

But my relief was short-lived.

I was ahead of Jibo and as we were passing an open door, I saw Mister Guga seated at a very large table with two hefty bodyguards standing behind him.

   I quickly passed the open door without being observed, but as Jibo was passing, Mister Guga saw him and started shouting,

   "Stop, Thief!

   "Stop, Thief!!"

   Jibo pushed me and said,

   "Hide Inca!

   Quick!

   Hide!

"Try to escape. I will manage on my own."

Seeing my reluctance to leave him, he pushed me gently and said sharply,

"Listen to me Inca, there's no time to hesitate. Hide!"

I quickly looked around and saw a heavy curtain. I quickly climbed up the curtain and hid on the top of it.

I looked down with dismay as the enormous men came crashing out of the room, while Madam Kira came from the other direction having been alerted by the loud noise made by Mister Guga.

Jibo was caught in the middle - -two thugs behind him and Madam Kira in front of him.

They didn't bother to look up. They thought that Jibo was alone.

Madam Kira shouted at Jibo,

"Give me that Egg!"

Jibo evaded her and dashed down the corridor with Madam Kira and the two goons running after him.

Jibo in his haste to get away slammed into a glass case housing some beautiful porcelain figurines. It fell with a loud "CRASH" shattering the glass and the figurines, leaving the place in a shamble!!

Mister Guga let out a loud howl of dismay when he saw the broken figurines on the floor.

Suddenly, Madam Kira let out a piercing whistle and who should arrive but the bratty Red Kites.

She started whispering to them and they gave chase to Jibo.

I watched helplessly. No one had spotted me. They were more concerned with chasing

Jibo, who was making a mad dash down the stairs crashing into and breaking more beautiful porcelain and furniture. Mister Guga howled like a wolf with a loud wail that could wake the dead.

The Red Kites continued to pursue Jibo who had arrived at the window. He swiftly flew out of it followed closely by the Red Kites.

Madam Kira, Mister Guga and the goons ran out of the mansion and jumped into a waiting car which pulled out of the grounds with a loud screech.

I clambered down the heavy curtain and avoiding the broken glass, sprinted to the ground floor and out of the open window from which Jibo had escaped.

I dashed to the rest of my team who were waiting for me, hidden behind a large bush on the grounds.

I gasped,

"HURRY!

"HURRY!!

"We need to follow Jibo and the Red Kites!!!"

There seemed to be hundreds of Red Kites! More had come to join the party and they all joined the chase.

We gasped in dismay!

Jibo was swallowed up by the Red Kites and when the air cleared, we found him without the bright Fabergé Egg!

The egg was now in the claws of two young
Red Kites who were speeding away with it.

The bratty Red Kites didn't seem to be too intelligent. Instead of returning to the mansion, they were heading in the opposite direction away from the mansion. They headed towards the River Neva.

We were trying our best to keep them in sight while on foot, by running through small alleys and avoiding the main roads. We came up to the bridge just as the big car carrying Mister Guga, his two goons and Madam Kira rolled up there as well.

Just then another noise rose above the howling of the wind and the cacophony of the Red Kites. We stopped in our tracks and looked up at the sky.

"R-r-r-r-r-r-r-r!

"R-r-r-r-r-r-r-r!!

"R-r-r-r-r-r-r-r!!!

"R-R-R-R-R-R-R-R-R-R-R-R-R-R!!!!

"R-R-R-R-R-R-R-R-R-R-R-R-R-R-R!!!!!

I looked up and saw that it was Jibo. He had turned himself in to the great black bird. He had not given up!

He pursued the two brats with great speed.

The noise seemed to rattle the Red Kites.

They looked around in confusion.

The Red Kites who had attacked the rabbits remembered their last experience with that sound and the great black bird they had encountered at the Peterhof palace gardens.

I saw Jibo soar up in the air above the two Red Kites and take a plunge from above. He crashed into the two Red Kites carrying the Egg.

The two Red Kites gave a loud squawk and dropped the Egg.

We watched in dismay as the wonderful Fabergé Egg descended and hit the water.

Madam Kira shrieked in anger and Mister Guga howled in horror while the two burly goons could do nothing but watch.

We looked up at Jibo wondering what he would do now. But it seemed that this was exactly what he had planned, knowing that the Red Kites would not venture into the chilly river to save the Egg.

He dived in after the Egg, deep into the River Neva and disappeared from sight.

Just then two large police cars pulled up on either side of the bridge.

Terrance barked,

"The cavalry arrives!"

Mister Guga's large car was on the bridge with the two police cars blocking him. He could not drive away.

There was pandemonium on the bridge! The driver of Mister Guga's car was unable to move.

We thought it best to withdraw from the scene after we saw Mister Guga, Madam Kira and the two goons being led away by the policemen.

154

30 September

Monday around 4.00 a.m. in the morning

It was dusk when we returned home. We were worried and concerned about our friend Jibo.

I fretted thinking - - -

Was Jibo alright?

Did a big nasty fish swallow him up??

Was he lost in the deep blue ocean???

Had we lost him to the deep Neva River????

Would he return to us ever again?????

What about the lovely Fabergé Egg??????

I suddenly realized that Jibo was more important to us than any Egg, valuable or not. If we had a choice over a very expensive Egg and Jibo, we would rather have dear little Jibo back.

Never mind the fabulous Egg!!

I gazed out of the window, longing to see Jibo's funny face again.

I swallowed my fears when I saw Cara in tears. She too, like the rest of us had grown very fond of Jibo.

Even our big and brave Terrance was really upset. He couldn't help but join Cara in shedding a tear.

We sat by the window, our eyes fixed on the River Neva, our hearts broken and sad.

I felt a deep sense of guilt coming on. If I had not ventured into this adventure, good-natured Jibo would still be with us.

With a heavy heart, I slowly walked into the

kitchen with the intention of hiding my head and having a good old bawl, away from the eyes of my team.

I entered the kitchen and got the shock of my life! There, sitting prettily on the kitchen counter, was the beautiful and fabulous Fabergé Egg.

I meowed out loud,

"HOW ON EARTH DID YOU GET HERE,

MR. EGG?"

No response from the egg of course, but on hearing my voice, the rest of the gang ran into the kitchen. They stood thunderstruck at the sight of the missing Fabergé Egg, sitting comfortably on top of the kitchen counter.

A sense of hope started creeping into my soul. The last person who had the Egg was of course Jibo. If the Egg was here, so was Jibo.

But where was he? I looked around eagerly - - - but no Jibo.

I meowed,

"Where is Jibo?"

Just as I was about to race around the apartment searching for Jibo, he casually floated into the kitchen.

We all shrieked with relief.

"Jibo where on earth have you been? We have been so worried about you." I meowed.

He calmly responded,

"I went to Moscow to check on Igor. He was sound asleep. He has no idea about what his sister has been up to."

Our sense of relief collectively gave way to delight and Jibo found himself surrounded by hugs and kisses, so much so, that his little two-sided face turned crimson with pleasure.

What an adventure!

Not only had we secured the missing Fabergé Egg, but the bad guys had been caught as well.

I thought smugly to myself that despite our team being short of two members, both Monk and Polo not having come with us to Russia, Inca & Company had done it again!!

"HURRAH!"

But I had to admit, that we would never have succeeded without Jibo. I was determined to nominate Jibo as an honorary member of Inca & Company.

So, I did, right there and then!

Monday morning Around 7.00 am

The sun had risen and our apartment was bathed in a soft golden light.

Jibo had gone back to the basement in Moscow. He had his morning duties. He had to wake Igor and give him his breakfast. He was Igor's companion and wanted to be there when Igor found out about his wayward sister, Madam Kira.

Jibo had already informed us that it was actually Madam Kira and Igor's father who had created Jibo. He had passed away peacefully soon after creating Jibo. He would have had no idea that his only daughter Kira would turn to crime.

But Jibo was not too concerned. He said he would remain with Igor. Jibo had enough brains and wisdom to protect and guide Igor. They had their lodgings and plenty of funds to live comfortably until Madam Kira returned, hopefully a changed person.

As daylight had set in, we flocked to the kitchen and waited for our breakfast.

More importantly we all wished to see Solo's reaction when he arrived in the kitchen to make his coffee and saw the fabulous Fabergé Egg sitting on the kitchen counter, ready to be picked up and admired.

Sharp at 7.00 a.m., Solo walked into the kitchen and bent down to fondle Terrance on the head and said good morning to all of us.

I wound myself around his ankles and meowed,

"Get us our breakfast,

"Hurry up, we deserve it after finding the missing Faberge Egg for you."

Of course, all he heard from three hungry cats was,

"MEOOW, MEOOOW and MEOOOOW!"

But when he turned around and saw the fabulous Egg sitting on the counter looking pretty and glittery, he forgot all about our food - - -

He stood stunned as he looked at the Egg.

He called out,

"Missy, Missy come look!

"Come quick!"

We looked at each other smugly while Mom came dashing out and both Solo and she stood gazing at the beautiful Egg.

Solo looked at us and said,

"Missy, let's say no more!

"I suspect our furry friends have been on another adventure.

"They deserve a special treat today!"

Soon after breakfast, Terrance and Solo raced off to the Fabergé Museum, taking the precious Egg with them. Solo was eager to hand it over to its rightful place.

It turned out that one of the goons working for Mister Guga was actually a secret police agent. He had called the police on the sly and that's why they had turned up so quickly. The police had been watching and waiting for the opportunity to catch Mister Guga and Madam Kira red-handed.

What an adventure! I couldn't wait to get back home and read my diary to Monk and Polo.

We were sad to leave Russia. Our plane was to leave Saint Petersburg that afternoon. Most of all, we were sad to leave Jibo. I wished he could come with us to London.

Jibo had put his heart and soul in helping us recover the missing Fabergé Egg.

When we expressed how we felt, Jibo had brushed it off. He said,

"My dear friends, I will visit you often. Now that I found you, how can I ever forget you? I promise you; you will see me soon!"

WHAT AN EXTRAORDINARY ADVENTURE!

CAT DETECTIVE SERIES

R.F. Kristi invites you to receive free books, news, and much more. Please sign up at:

www.incabookseries.com

INCA
CAT DETECTIVE SERIES

- **The Cats Who Crossed Over from Paris**

- **Christmas Cats**

- **Cats in Provence**

- **Ninja Spy Cats**

- **Diary of a Snoopy Cat (available in Chinese and Spanish)**

- **Vampires at Easter (Diary of a Snoopy Cat)**

- **Serendipity Mystery (Diary of a Snoopy Cat) - (available in Chinese, German and Spanish)**

- **Cats in the Korean Peninsula (Diary of a Snoopy Cat)**

- **The Cat Detectives in Russia: The Case of the Missing Fabergé Egg (Diary of a Snoopy Cat)**

R.F. KRISTI's INCA CAT DETECTIVE SERIES

Winner in the Wishing Shelf Book Awards & Reader's Favorite Awards

"The Verdict: It's pretty easy to recommend the Inca Book Series. The books are fun, interesting, and well-illustrated, and provide a great deal of value. The characters are fantastic and the stories are even better. The French cultural influence is a real positive for me as well, because that's such a rarity and I think it's great for kids to learn about other countries and cultures. The Illustrations:

...The illustrations rank right up there...the characters are all incredibly cute and the style of these illustrations is unique. I can't think of another book we've reviewed here at Kids Fun Channel that looks anything like this. I simply love the cats, their expressions, and how much these illustrations add to the fun found in this book."

Kids Fun Channel

QUIZ TIME:

Connect via:

www.incabookseries.com

If you enjoy this book, please leave a review
on Amazon or Goodreads.
Positive reviews help a great deal.

Thank you

Made in the USA
Monee, IL
04 August 2021